CW00502776

KLAUS HAAPANIEMI

with stories by Rosa Liksom

POCKO

A CPI record for this book is available from the British Library.

All stories except "Tampere" written
by Rosa Liksom
©2004 Rosa Liksom
Translated from Finnish to English
by Hilkka Rocosa
All photographs except pages 43 - 45
by Matti Pyykkö
Direction for layout
Mia Wallenius

Edited by Nicola Schwartz
Design by Olga Norman
assisted by Cristina Redondo
Foreword by Marc Hulson
Cover text by Lucien Rothenstein

*

Published by
Pocko Editions
PO Box 20190
London W10 5LA
Phone +44 (0)20 8964 9580
Fax +44 (0)20 8964 9580
info@pocko.com
www.pocko.com
ISBN: 1-903977-25-8

First published in the United States by
Gingko Press Inc.
5768 Paradise Drive, Suite J
Corte Madera, CA 94925, USA
Phone 415 924 9615
Fax 415 924 9608
books@gingkopress.com
www.gingkopress.com
ISBN: 1-58423-179-3

❦ FOREWORD ❦

Perhaps it is the very wilderness of the local landscape that invokes the vividness of Scandinavian folklore: the extremity of the seasons - the awesome, terrifying proximity of nature - conjures up a magical parallel universe populated by worms, demons, trolls and monsters. The Finnish illustrator and graphic designer Klaus Haapaniemi embraces the pagan mysticism of his native culture, but instills it with a distinctly contemporary twist.

In Haapaniemi's immersive, hallucinogenic universe, a megalomaniac graphic decorator with an unhinged baroque imagination appears to have been let loose on the natural world. God has fallen asleep and all manner of garish, hybrid creatures run amuck, spreading a riot of pattern and psychedelia behind them. Everything in these landscapes is in a state of continual flux or transformation. The anthropomorphic visual play approaches a point of extremity where individual motifs defy verbal description: as the reader contemplates a liquid yellow cloud, grinning insanely, drifting past green-turreted, moustachioed trolls, language gives up the ghost.

This is both an antidote to the saccharin fantasies of Disneyesque visions of nature, and at the same time refreshingly unaffected by the cynicism and irony that characterises much so-called alternative contemporary illustration. There is a radical innocence about Haapaniemi's vision: one imagines the makers of the Magic Roundabout restaging Bosch's Garden of Earthly Delights, the surrealist whimsy of the former tempering the disturbing apparitions of the latter.

For this edition the best-selling Finnish novelist Rosa Liksom has written a short story inspired by Haapaniemi's imagery. Rather than attempt the impossible task of literally narrating the hallucinatory visual excess of the illustrations, the magical realism of the text works as a more naturalistic literary accompaniment.

by **Rosa Liksom**

*I wake up before the sun. The moonlight sweeps a dark path
in the middle of the room for the ants to walk. I lean my head
against the cool window. In the sky, glowing green constellations;
in the snow; the stickiness of the thaw, the immense silence of
the universe over the small village. This is my world: far away
the road, trembling under the weight of eighteen-wheelers, close
by the lake that reflects the sky with white clouds and the forest
that is dimly visible in the icy sparkling fog. Mom wakes up
before the others. She lights the fire in the stove and puts the
coffeepot on to bubble. She clatters while going down the attic
stairs. She clears her throat at the door and sits on the bench
to browse through yesterday's newspaper. In the living room,
grandma turns over in her iron bed and groans in a faint voice.*

I ski through the wild garden behind the cottage to the river bank. The sky is clear and fresh. At the mouth of the river the water foams and casts heavy steam clouds into the frosty air. It is sacred and terrifying. Nobody defies its strength, not even in the summer, when its water has run short and the current is light. I move along the rocky river bank towards the mouth of the river as I want to see it with my own eyes, the ski track that starts from the house and disappears in the dark water. There was a path from here, used once, but the flurry of snow has covered it, as if it was a memory of Pearl who never existed.

And then I saw it. It rose in the middle of the pine forest, round and all-knowing. Like an old and ruddy friend. I took off my skis and sank deeply into the frozen snow. I stamped a crunchy path around it. It was the perfect height, like a breast to suck in the emptiness of space.

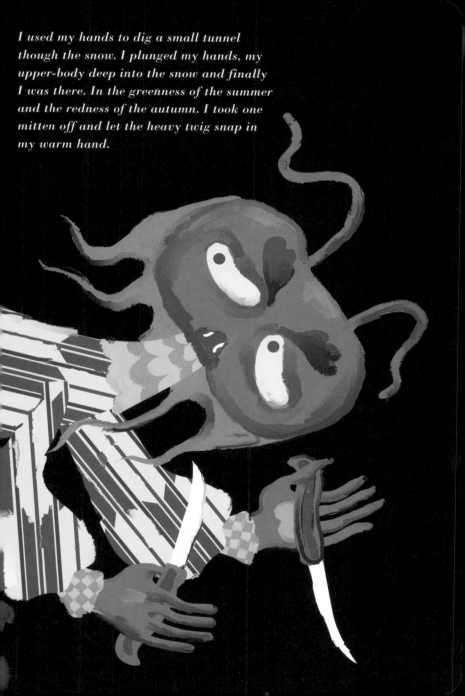

I used my hands to dig a small tunnel though the snow. I plunged my hands, my upper-body deep into the snow and finally I was there. In the greenness of the summer and the redness of the autumn. I took one mitten off and let the heavy twig snap in my warm hand.

The juicy lingonberries melted into life and started shining like forged steel. I dug a hole around it and freed the whole clump of red earth from the weight of the lifeless snow. I took the whole thing in my arms. The blood of the berries, the whiteness of the snow and the sky, as they should be.

I put on my skis and my mittens and then it happened. Little birds, numb from coldness, flocked over my head, flew round the rowan tree right to the clump and disappeared silently into the bowels of the earth.

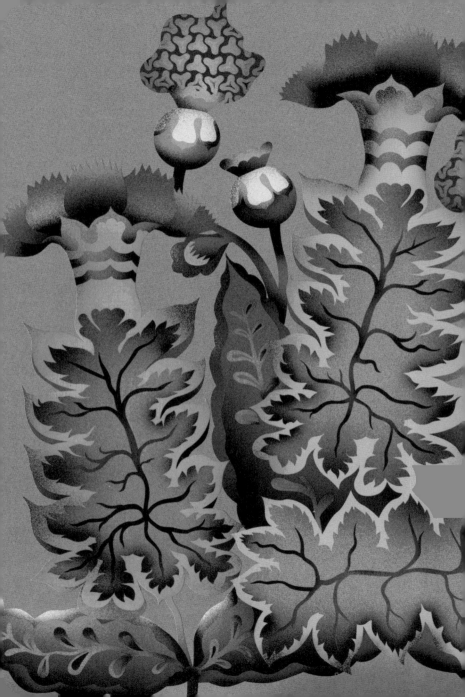

The boy made the fire.
He stamped a deep hole in
the soft snow and made a camp-
fire. He filled it with birch bark,
struck the match. The wood took
the fire and warmed the heavy
trunk of a nearby spruce.
The birch bark crackled
like firecrackers.

Behind the willow there was a hole in the ice from the day before, but it had frozen over during the night. I took an axe from my backpack and cut the hole open, my icy spit freezing and ricocheting off.

The boy had taken off his clothes and piled
them neatly up on top of the firewood.
He walked behind me, unsteadily,
to the hole. He laughed and dropped
into the jagged edged eye of the ice.
His childish behaviour frightened me.

The sun was glistening behind the pine forest.
I quickly took my clothes off. I threw them
in a messy bundle at the edge of the
hole and jumped into the water.
The blood exploded in my veins
and tingled on the top of my head.
There were many trees and we weren't
in a hurry. The boy was looking at the red
snow drifts rising on the opposite shore.
It would be a mild night

They peeped out from behind two spruces. Two women who were skiing side by side, slowly, directly towards me. I leaned my head against the rough icy bark of the spruce. A warm heart was beating inside the tree. The branches were heavy under the weight of the snow. They were bending and creaking in the land of silence.

I squinted to see them better.
One of them was wearing a long
black overcoat and the other one
had a bright red woollen hat.
I recognized them. How innocent
and virtuous these women looked
on the garish white snow.
They went round the
snowdrifts on the ice
and made their way
to the edge of the
forest. They would
sense me when
they came ashore.

I grabbed the trunk of the spruce with both hands and pressed my ear against it. Secret dozing life, please answer me.

During the night the sandstorm got out of
control and covered the sauna, the potato
cellar, the playhouse and the sheep shed.
In the morning light Ilmari dug the sheep
shed out. First, a deep hole where the door
was supposed to be. The sand was easy to
move. It was warm as it had come from
south, but then it had cooled down just
enough in the frozen hours after midnight.
Then, the south-facing window. The sheep
greeted the first ray of light as though it
were their keeper bringing them fresh water
just before sunrise.

He left the playhouse, and the potato cellar could wait, too.
Ilmari stepped on the roof of the sauna in his Wellingtons and looked
at the pine in front of the sauna. Its heavy branches were bending
under the weight of the reddish sand; they creaked when Ilmari
touched them lightly.

He had to start again from the door. Ilmari stuck the spade into the sand crystallized by ice, and smiled. How clean the world was, how silent and sincere.

He dug the tunnel downwards and continued along the wall of the
sauna with the door in it. The heavy spade hit the upper frame of
the door. Ilmari laughed and wiped sweat from his forehead. He was
deep in the tunnel and saw the blue sky, fluffy clouds and the sun
sparkling high in the sky. It could have been a sweltering summer day.

The vertical tunnel reached from the eaves of the sauna to the thresh-
old of the door. Ilmari had achieved the first stage. He lifted the spade
in the air and waved it. It was like greeting the universe from the
depth of the ground. He didn't even try to open the door as there was
very little space.

Another tunnel had to be dug, first straight and then slightly upwards. Four thrusts into the dense sand with a drain spade, a gentle touch and a cube of earth formed perfectly in front of Ilmari. He had done this hundreds of times. There was a mellow silence in the sand tunnel, like at the bottom of the sea.

Just one more thrust and the sun dazzled
him. Ilmari sat down and sunk deep
into the sand softened by the
morning sun; he sniffled
and winked at the
plump red sun.

The door of the sauna was stuck. A little hit with the spade, a pull and the door clinked open like an egg breaking.

The window was full of fine sand. The wooden floor creaked under
Ilmari's feet in a familiar way. He sat on a stool and drew his mark
on the window with saliva. The bright dawn of the day came far
away from the end of the tunnel into the changing room of the sauna.
It was dark in the sauna. It smelled of smoke and soap. Ilmari turned
on his torch, carried an armful of birch wood and dry birch bark
from the entrance to the stove.

*First he had to light the fire in the sauna stove and then bring water
from the cowshed to the water boiler and after that light a fire under
the boiler. Ilmari sat on the sauna bench and watched the fire so
long that the sauna stove began to sizzle and the water
in the boiler started to steam. He took off his
clothes in the changing room. The floor
was cold and the walls were damp.*

By the light of a bulb Ilmari climbed up to the top bench, slowly threw water onto the heated rocks and yawned with satisfaction. He used a birch switch to get rid of demons and worms, crept into the blue afternoon, rolled in the sand, making the angel Gabriel with his hands, and arms and scowled at the cooling sun.

He came back to the top bench, cautiously threw water onto the rocks. Ilmari lay down, lifted his feet towards the ceiling and shut his eyes. How wrong his dreams had been, how perfect was life in itself; the exploding village touched by the sun, the white columns of smoke, the beauty and the suffering that came with it, to which he was condemned.

TAMPERE

TAMPERE IS A PLACE WHERE SKYSCRAPERS CAST SHADOWS OVER STEAMBOATS SAILING IN THE BEAUTI-
FUL SURROUNDING LAKES. THE SAILORS SMILE AND GAY MEN ALL HAVE A GLIMMER IN THEIR EYE. IF YOU
OBSERVE THE STREETS OF TAMPERE. YOU WILL SEE TROLLS, COWBOYS, ROLE-PLAYERS AND HAPPY
LEATHER MEN STROLLING AROUND TOGETHER IN PEACEFUL HEGEMONY. MOUNTAINS DISAPPEAR BEHIND
TALL BUILDINGS AND A WIND BLOWS THE RESTLESSNESS AWAY FROM TRAVELLERS' HEARTS...HERE IN THE
CHICAGO OF FINLAND.

✧ THE AUTHOR ✧

In summer of 1992, Klaus and I attended confirmation camp
where religion is coerced into the minds of Finnish teenagers.
During the evenings we listened to the priest's stories about sin
but in secret we doodled pictures of the devil.

One day we wandered into the Kalevala woods to look for Forest Gods.
Before the Christian crusades in the Middle Ages,
all Finnish people had faith in the divinity of Nature.
Klaus and I wanted to rediscover that same beauty
in nature for our own lives.

Klaus fell in love with the Karelian landscape and had an epiphany.
After our journey he adopted a more tranquil style
and he began to plan his production
so he could access as large an audience as possible.

Klaus has something like a "virgin" mind,
whose adolescence was fortunately untouched
by all the filth floating around us.
Klaus built his own environment
which we can now experience
through his work.

Let me introduce you to:
Klaus Haapaniemi!

Matti Pyykkö
Curator